MARK HANKINS

LOVE

THE SECRET TO

SUCCESS

MARK HANKINS

LOVE
THE SECRET TO
SUCCESS

Unless otherwise indicated, all scriptural quotations are from the King James Version of the Bible.

Love: The Secret of Success
ISBN #9781889981604

Published by:
Mark Hankins Ministries Publications
P.O. Box 12863
Alexandria, LA 71315
318.767.2001
www.markhankins.org

Table of Contents

Love: The Secret To Success

We must renew our minds daily in the scriptures about the God-kind of love. This will bring our thoughts into agreement with the love that is already in our heart. When we know God's love for us, God's love in us – it is easy to love others. Like a mother smiles her baby into smiling, God loves us into loving and gives us into giving.

This is the way God loves us and it is the way He expects us to love others. **Walking in the God-kind of love is our greatest challenge. It is also our greatest reward.** God not only commands us to love one another but He has given us the love to do it with – it's in our hearts.

The greatest miracle and witness to the world in the last days is for Christians to have this kind of love for one another. Jesus said in John 13:34 – 35, *"A new*

commandment I give unto you, that you love one another; as I have loved you, that you also love one another. By this shall all men know that you are my disciples, if you have love one to another." God's love gives us the power and authority to demonstrate God's mercy to others, just as Jesus did on the cross when He prayed to His Father to forgive. It is God's love in action.

Henry Drummond said, "You will find, if you think for a moment, that the people who influence you are people who believe in you. In an atmosphere of suspicion men shrivel up, but in a trusting atmosphere they expand, and find encouragement and educative fellowship. The possession of it is the great secret of personal influence."

1 Corinthians 13:4-8 is a definition of the love of God. As we meditate on the love of God by affirming it out loud and using our imagination to see ourselves, others and situations we're facing in the light of His love, we are renewing our minds and feeding our faith!

The love of God...
possession of it is
THE GREAT SECRET
of personal influence.

— henry drummond

1 CORINTHIANS 13:4-8 (KJV)

Charity* suffereth long, and is kind; charity envieth not; charity vaunteth not itself, is not puffed up, ***Doth not behave itself unseemly,*** seeketh not her own, is not easily provoked, thinketh no evil; Rejoiceth not in iniquity, but rejoiceth in the truth; Beareth all things, believeth all things, hopeth all things, endureth all things. Charity never faileth...

*Charity is translated as *agape*. Agape means "the God-kind of love."

anytime you are
FEELING MISTREATED
you know the devil is
WORKING ON YOU!

-kenneth e. hagin

if you aren't
THINKING the way
≡LOVE THINKETH≡
it won't be long
before you are not
ACTING the way
LOVE ACTETH!

—Mark Hankins

1 CORINTHIANS 13:4-8 (AMP)

Love endures long and is patient and kind; love never is envious nor boils over with jealousy; is not boastful or vainglorious, does not display itself haughtily. It is not conceited (arrogant and inflated with pride); it is not rude (unmannerly) and does not act unbecomingly. *Love (God's love in us) does not insist on its own rights or its own way, for it is not selfseeking; it is not touchy or fretful or resentful; it takes no account of the evil done to it [it pays no attention to a suffered wrong].* It does not rejoice at injustice and unrighteousness, but rejoices when right and truth prevail. Love bears up under anything and everything that comes, *is ever ready to believe the best of every person,* its hopes are fadeless under all circumstances, and it endures everything [without weakening]. Love never fails [never fades out or becomes obsolete or comes to an end].

1 CORINTHIANS 13:4-8 (JORDAN)

...Love is not envious, nor does it strut and brag. It does not act up, nor try to get things for itself. *It pitches no tantrums, keeps no books on insults or injuries,* sees no fun in wickedness, but rejoices when truth prevails. Love is all-embracing, all-trusting, all-hoping, all-enduring. Love never quits...

The moments
you have
REALLY LIVED
in life, will be the
moments you have
REALLY LOVED.

— henry drummond

1 CORINTHIANS 13:4-8 (HAYFORD)

Love suffers long, having patience with imperfect people. Love is kind, and active in doing good. *Love does not envy; since it is non-possessive and non-competitive, it actually wants others to get ahead.* Hence it does not parade itself. Love has a self-effacing quality; it is not ostentatious. Love is not puffed up, treating others arrogantly; it does not behave rudely, but displays good manners and courtesy. Love does not seek its own, insisting on its own rights and demanding precedence; rather, it is unselfish. *Love is not provoked; it is not irritable or touchy, rough or hostile, but is graceful under pressure.* Love thinks no evil; it does not keep an account of wrongs done to it; instead it erases resentments. Love does not rejoice in iniquity, finding satisfaction in the shortcomings of others and spreading an evil report; rather, it rejoices in the truth, aggressively advertising the good. Love bears all things, defending and holding other people up. Love believes the best about others, credits them with good intentions, and is not suspicious. *Love hopes all things, never giving up on people, but affirming their future.* Love endures all things, persevering and remaining loyal to the end.

you can't
GROW IN GOD
without growing
IN LOVE.

—mark hankins

1 CORINTHIANS 13:4-8 (PHIL.)

This love of which I speak is slow to lose patience - it looks for a way of being constructive. It is not possessive: *it is neither anxious to impress nor does it cherish inflated ideas of its own importance.* Love has good manners and does not pursue selfish advantage. It is not touchy. It does not keep account of evil or gloat over the wickedness of other people. Love knows no limit to its endurance, no end to its trust, no fading of its hope; it can outlast anything. It is, in fact, the one thing that still stands when all else has fallen.

1 CORINTHIANS 13:4-8 (WMS.)

Love is so patient and so kind; Love never boils with jealousy; It never boasts, is never puffed with pride; It does not act with rudeness, or insist upon its rights; *It never gets provoked, it never harbors evil thoughts;* Is never glad when wrong is done, But always glad when truth prevails; It bears up under anything, *It exercises faith in everything,* It keeps up hope in everything, It gives us power to endure in anything.

you will give
yourself
To MANY THINGS,
give yourself
FIRST to love.

-henry drummond

a step out
OF LOVE
is a step out
OF GOD.

-kenneth e. hagin
1 JOHN 4:16

1 CORINTHIANS 13:4-8 (WUEST)

*Love meekly and patiently bears ill treatment from others. Love is kind, gentle, benign, pervading and penetrating the whole nature, mellowing all which would have been harsh and austere....*Love does not brag, nor does it show itself off...does not have an inflated ego...is not irritated, provoked, exasperated, aroused to anger...

1 CORINTHIANS 13:4-8 (MSG)

Love never gives up. Love cares more for others than for self. Love doesn't want what it doesn't have. Love doesn't strut, Doesn't have a swelled head, ***Doesn't force itself on others, Isn't always "me first," Doesn't fly off the handle,*** Doesn't keep score of the sins of others, Doesn't revel when others grovel, Takes pleasure in the flowering of truth, Puts up with anything, Trusts God always, ***Always looks for the best, Never looks back, But keeps going to the end.*** Love never dies.

To love
ABUNDANTLY
is to live abundantly,
& to love forever is
TO LIVE FOREVER.
Hence, eternal life is
INEXTRICABLY
bound up with love.

-henry drummond

WALKING
in the GOD-KIND
of love is your
GREATEST
CHALLENGE.
it is also your
GREATEST
REWARD.

—mark hankins

1 CORINTHIANS 13:4-8 (BARCLAY)

Love is patient with people; love is kind....Love never does the graceless thing; never insists on its rights, never irritably loses its temper; never nurses its wrath to keep it warm. Love finds nothing to be glad about when someone goes wrong....Love can stand any kind of treatment; *love's first instinct is to believe in people; love never regards anyone or anything as hopeless;* nothing can happen that can break love's spirit. Love lasts forever.

1 CORINTHIANS 13:4-8 (TLB)

Love does not demand its own way. It is not irritable or touchy. It does not hold grudges and will hardly even notice when others do it wrong. It is never glad about injustice, but rejoices whenever truth wins out. If you love someone you will be loyal to him no matter what the cost. You will always believe in him, always expect the best of him, and always stand your ground in defending him.

You may be
ABLE TO
whip a skunk,
but you might not
WANT TO

−Mark hankins
MARK 11:25

≡ THE FIRST ≡
evidence that we're
a child of God is
WALKING IN LOVE!

—Mark Hankins

1 CORINTHIANS 13:4-8 (JOHNSON)

Let me describe love. Love stays in difficult relationships with kindness. *Love does not play "one-up-man-ship," nor does it react to those who do. Love is not rude or grasping or overly sensitive, nor does love search for imperfections and faults in others.* Love is the most enduring quality of human existence. It keeps on keeping on; it trusts in God in every situation and expects God to act in all circumstances. Nothing can destroy love.

1 CORINTHIANS 13:4-8 (TPT)

Love is large and incredibly patient. Love is gentle and consistently kind to all. It refuses to be jealous when blessing comes to someone else. Love does not brag about one's achievements nor inflate its own importance. *Love does not traffic in shame and disrespect, nor selfishly seek its own honor.* Love is not easily irritated or quick to take offense. Love joyfully celebrates honesty and finds no delight in what is wrong. Love is a safe place of shelter, for it never stops believing the best for others. *Love never takes failure as defeat, for it never gives up.*

The world is not
a playground;
it is a SCHOOLROOM.
life is not a holiday,
but an EDUCATION,
& one eternal lesson
for us all is how better
CAN WE LOVE.

— henry drummond

like a mother
SMILES her baby
into smiling, God
loves us into
≡ LOVING ≡
& gives us into
GIVING.

—mark hankins

The Way God Loves

And we have known and believed the love that God hath to us. God is love; and he that dwelleth in love dwelleth in God, and God in him.

1 John 4:16

Jackie Robinson, the first African American to play professional baseball, joined the Dodgers in 1947. He traveled with them during their first road trip and was heckled by fans in Cincinnati, Ohio. During pre-game in field practice, Reese, the captain of the team, went over to Robinson and engaged him in conversation. He put his arm around his shoulder in a gesture of support which silenced the crowd. That event was the turning point of Jackie's famous career.

In the same way, the Apostle Paul experienced public ridicule and rejection when everyone forsook him. That's when he said in 2 Timothy 4:17, "The Lord stood by me and strengthened me." That is the way God loves.

The greatest miracle and witness to the world in the last days is for Christians to have this kind of love for one another. Jesus said in John 13:34,35, "***A new commandment I give unto you, that you love one another; as I have loved you, that you also love one another. By this shall all men know that you are my disciples, if you have love one to another.***" God's love gives you the power and authority to demonstrate God's mercy to others, just as Jesus did on the cross when He prayed to His Father to forgive. It is God's love in action.

LOVE LIKE HE LOVES

If ye fulfill the royal law of scripture, Thou shalt love thy neighbor as thyself, ye do

well...and mercy rejoiceth over judgment.
James 2:8,13

Love comes from God and everyone in His family can love like He loves because we share His nature (1 John 4:7-8). Never underestimate the reach of God's mercy as demonstrated when Jesus forgave the thief on the cross. Love restored the woman caught in the act of adultery. Religion would have killed her, but instead of throwing rocks, Jesus bent down, wrote in the sand and her accusers had to walk away. Mercy triumphed over judgment and is the standard for us to follow.

When I was a teenager, I had an encounter with the love of God that changed the direction of my life. I was sitting in church on a Sunday morning after being out on Saturday night with my friends. I was not exactly living right; in fact, I was backslidden. In the middle of the service, a man named Bro. F.E. Ward stepped up to the platform and said he had a word from God for someone. Well, that someone happened to be me! My friend next to me whispered, "You're a dead duck now." As I walked to the front I began to repent of my sins. I reminded God that if He revealed them, my father would kill me, and I would be of no use to Him then. Instead of a giant flyswatter coming to squash me from Heaven, Bro. Ward began to tell me how much God loved me and how He had a plan for my life. Immediately all the rebellion melted and I received direction for my life that day. If He loves us like this, we can love others in the same way.

GOD'S DEFINITION OF LOVE

Love endures long and is patient and kind; love never is envious nor boils over with jealousy, is not boastful or vainglorious, does not display itself haughtily. It is not conceited (arrogant and inflated with pride); it is not rude (unmannerly) and does not act unbecomingly. Love (God's love in us) does not insist on its own rights or its own way, for it is not self-seeking; it is not touchy or fretful or resentful; it takes no account of the evil done to it [it pays no attention to a suffered wrong]. It does not rejoice at injustice and unrighteousness but rejoices when right and truth prevail. Love bears up under anything and everything that comes, is ever ready to believe the best of every person, its hopes are fadeless under all circumstances, and it endures everything [without weakening]. Love never fails [never fades out or becomes obsolete or comes to an end].

1 Corinthians 13:4-8 (AMP)

There are nine aspects of the love of God which can be described as light shining through a prism and dividing into many colors. **PATIENT**: First of all, love is grace for imperfect people. Love is not in a hurry but is persistent and prepared to wait. It is graceful under preasure. **KIND**: The best thing you can do for God is to be kind to His kids! You can't love the Father and not love His children. Acts of kindness and love communicate happiness to those around us. **NOT ENVIOUS:** Love prefers others, is not competitive but is generous. In any line of work, there will be others who are better, and it is a temptation to push others down in order to get ahead. But love will help others to be their best, preferring them first. **HUMBLE:** Jesus did not seek His own honor but allowed God to honor Him. When you do a kind deed, humility is quiet, not bringing attention to itself. **COURTEOUS:** Love does the mannerly thing. Anyone, no matter the level of their education or culture, will be gracious when they walk in love. Love speaks the truth gently. **UNSELFISH:** It is not grasping but generous, knowing it is more blessed to give than to receive. It is not stingy, but ready to share, given to hospitality. **NOT EASILY PROVOKED:** Love does not have a bad temper. Great talents and influence can be completely destroyed in one fit of anger. There are sins of the body and sins of the disposition. For example, the sin of the prodigal son's older brother was greater because he was ungrateful for his father's constant provision and jealous of his brother's honor. **GUILELESS AND SINCERE:** Love does not find satisfaction in the shortcomings of others and it does not spread an evil report. It aggressively advertises the good in people; it defends and holds other people up, credits them with good intentions and is not suspicious. It never gives up on people but affirms and encourages them.

HOW TO WALK IN GOD'S KIND OF LOVE

When you see how much God loves you, you can forgive yourself and you can also forgive others. By doing this you release yourself and others from past hurts, sins, and disappointments. Unforgiveness can open the door to sickness and the thief who comes to steal, kill, and destroy. Be quick to repent, quick to forgive, and quick to believe!

The next thing is to keep looking into the perfect law of liberty. James 1:25 (NLB) says, "But if you look carefully into the perfect law that sets you free, and if you do what it says and don't forget what you heard, then God will bless you for doing it." Renew your mind and feed your faith by meditating on this topic. This involves affirming it out loud and also using your imagination to see yourself, others, and situations you're facing in the light of God's love.

The third exercise to strengthen your love walk is to pray in the Spirit. ***"But ye beloved, building up yourselves on your most holy faith, praying in the Holy Ghost, keep yourselves in the love of God...,"*** Jude 20-21. This spiritual exercise involves yielding the most unruly member of your body to the Holy Spirit, who makes us holy. "...The love of God is shed abroad in our hearts by the Holy Spirit which is given unto us," Romans 5:5. He is the Greater One who will help you to tame your tongue, which is like a wild animal that cannot be domesticated! The tongue must be continually yielded to the power of the Holy Spirit who gives us power to overcome.

MAKE GOD'S LOVE YOUR QUEST

*Go after a life of love as if your life depended
on it, because it does.*

1 Corinthians 14:1 (Message)

*Eagerly pursue and seek to acquire [this]
love [make it your aim, your great quest].*

(Amplified)

A quest is a lifelong dream or anything that
dominates your life and holds your attention for at least
20 years. As believers our great quest in life should be
making the daily decision to walk in the God of love.
It is not a waste of time and it is a necessity to inspect
our love walk on a continual basis so the power that
raised Jesus from the dead may flow unhindered. Faith
works by love and when we make it our quest, we'll
see the worst people and situations turn around, and
experience favor, promotion, and Heaven on earth!

If you are going
To be a (forgiven)
person, you will
have To be a
(forgiving)
person.

Mark Hankins
Mark 11:25-26

You May Be Able To Whip A Skunk But You Might Not Want To

These words were spoken to me by an experienced "old timer" preacher. I felt mistreated and was complaining to this minister about some friends who had done me wrong. I wanted to get even with these people, and I was sure this minister would understand. As I explained my situation, this minister said these powerful words that I have never forgotten: "You may be able to whip a skunk, but you might not want to." Anytime I want to get back at someone I always remember that skunk.

The first step to walking in God's love is to forgive. "Therefore, be imitators of God as dear children. And walk in love, as Christ also has loved us and given

Himself for us..." Eph. 5:1-2. God's love nature is in you and He would not require you to do something you couldn't do. God is faithful and just to forgive our sins so, like Him, we can forgive. Then we are in position to receive forgiveness, mercy, and answers to our prayers.

OUGHT REMOVER

Jesus said in Mark 11:25, "And when ye stand praying, forgive, if ye have ought against any." An ought is any little thing. People say, "You ought to or ought not have done this." Instead, Jesus said to forgive so that your Father in heaven can forgive you. I sometimes think it would be good to spray some people down with ought remover! Jesus said you can forgive while you stand praying. It can be that quick! Don't say it's going to take time to get over your offense. ***Time doesn't enable you to get over your hurt, only choosing to forgive does.***

THE COST OF UNFORGIVENESS

In Luke 17:1-6, Jesus taught the disciples to forgive, even up to seventy times seven times each day. He also talked about the sycamine tree and how they could use their authority to command the tree to be uprooted and planted in the sea. The sycamine tree actually represents offense. Here are five amazing facts about sycamine trees: 1) they grow in dry places 2) the roots grow deep 3) the fruit is very bitter and is eaten by the poor 4) the wood is used for building coffins 5) they are pollinated by the stinger of a wasp.

Unforgiveness puts us in a spiritually dry place where Satan can find an entrance into our lives (Matthew 12:43). Unforgiveness and bitterness grow deep roots that not only take over your life, but defile others as well (Hebrews 12:15). As believers, we have the authority to speak to challenging places of offense in our life and they have to be planted in the sea. The wonderful thing about the sea is that it has the capacity to dissolve all bitterness and hurt so they are completely forgotten.

IT PAYS TO FORGIVE

Dad Hagin told a story about a lady whose daughter had epilepsy. After spending some time with her, he found out that she had bitterness toward her mother-in-law. She actually confessed to him, "I hate my mother-in-law." Dad Hagin explained to her 1 John 3:15 says that if you hate your brother, you're a murderer. He asked her to say those words again and asked her to listen down on the inside this time. So, she said them again and described that she felt a little scratch inside. Dad Hagin told her that scratch was the Holy Spirit trying to get her attention. He instructed her to act like she would if she did love her mother-in-law, because she did. This lady forgave her mother-in-law and began to pray for her. The little girl was fine until a few days later when she suffered another seizure. This time the mother simply said, "Satan, I'm walking in love. Take your hands off my child." The seizure stopped and the girl never again suffered another attack.

I remember going to one of Dad Hagin's meetings expecting to hear about his visions and latest revelations from God. Instead, he preached a message about forgiveness and walking in the God kind of love. I thought, "That is not my problem." As he continued preaching, I realized I did indeed have a problem with unforgiveness. At the end of the service, he called for those who needed to repent to stand to their feet. I was sitting in the minister's section and thought, "There is no way I am going to do that – that would be embarrassing." But I knew I needed to respond so I stood up, repented and decided, "I'm going to walk in love whether anyone else does or not."

It was a small adjustment, but it made a big difference. In fact, in just 30 days, I was out of debt as a direct result of my decision to forgive and to walk in the love of God. Does it pay to forgive? Yes, it does! Faith works by love.

I decided I'm going to walk walk in *LOVE* whether anyone else does or not.

Rev. Kenneth E. Hagin

Seventy Times Seven

*"He who refuses to forgive, burns the bridge
over which he himself must pass."*

Have you ever studied the New Testament on the subject of forgiveness? The radical kind of forgiveness that God extends to us is the same kind He expects us to extend to others. It is amazing how in Christian circles we can rejoice about God's forgiveness to us and have a brother by the throat at the same time.

One of the most important lessons we can learn in life is how to forgive. In Luke 17:1-6, Jesus commanded forgiveness not seven times, not seventy times but seventy times seven! God expects us to forgive our brother four hundred ninety times. Perhaps God is so serious about us forgiving others because of the radical forgiveness He has extended to us (Psalm 103:1-3). God forgives and forgets our sins and expects us to do the same (Isaiah 43:25-26).

The Greek meaning for the word forgive includes these words: forsake, leave, let go, and remit. It denotes a cessation and completion. That means it is in the past and should be forgotten. It is over. When we refuse to forgive, we destroy the bridge we must cross to reach our blessing and destiny. Forgiveness is always connected to receiving God's best blessings. Joseph forgave his brothers and reached his destiny. Satan always means it for evil, but God will turn it for good (Genesis 50:20).

> *And the Lord turned the captivity of Job,*
> *when he prayed for his friends: also the*
> *Lord gave Job twice as much as he had*
> *before.*
>
> *Job 42:10*

Job prayed for his persecutors and critics. When he exercised love and forgiveness, there was a turn for the better in his condition. Forgiveness is always a turning point. Job was able to turn things around in his life by forgiving and you can too!

CHOOSE TO FORGIVE

Praying for those who have hurt you or wronged you is choosing to forgive. The first lesson Jesus gave about prayer in the New Testament is about forgiveness. *"Love your enemies, bless them that curse you, do good to them that hate you, and pray for them that despitefully use you, and persecute you; that you may be the children of your Father which is in Heaven,"* Matthew 5:44-45.

As I mentioned in the previous chapter, I had complained to an older minister about some "friends" who had done me wrong. I felt mistreated and wanted some payback or revenge. I felt justified in my feelings and was offended. As I explained the situation to this older minister he said, "You may be able to whip a skunk, but you might not want to." I have never forgotten that statement. Any time I want to get back at someone, I always remember the skunk.

UNFORGIVENESS

The smell of unforgiveness defiles the atmosphere in every area of our lives. Unforgiveness is worse than the smell; it is a deadly poison that can kill. Forgiveness enables us to escape the "stink" that Satan is trying to put on us.

I heard Dad Hagin say, *"Any time you feel mistreated, you know the devil is working on you."* Satan is a master of offense. He is the accuser of the brethren. When we judge others, we are allowing Satan to use our mouths. Dad Hagin also said, "Putting out another fellow's candle doesn't brighten our own."

FAITH'S GREATEST ENEMY

After the powerful lessons on unlimited faith and receiving from God in Mark 11:23-24, Jesus warns about unforgiveness (vs. 25). *The greatest enemy to faith is unforgiveness.* Unforgiveness stops faith from working, hinders your prayer life, limits blessing, stops spiritual growth, opens the door to the devil, and can cause sickness and disease – even premature death. Unforgiveness is a killer. Holding or nursing grudges - large or small - is a killer (Ephesians 4:26-27).

GET RID OF OUGHT

When you stand praying, forgive, if you have ought against any.... Mark 11:25

Jesus said if you have ought against any. This word ought simply means any little thing. It is wrong to hold unforgiveness against others or even against yourself. If Jesus says you are forgiven, then you need to believe it, receive it, and expect God's best blessings from now on. It does not take ten years to forgive. Jesus said you can choose to forgive when you stand praying. It takes less than ten seconds to forgive. Harboring unforgiveness can spoil ten years of your life.

we love OTHERS,
we love EVERYBODY,
we love our ENEMIES,
because He
FIRST LOVED US.

- henry drummond

All is Forgiven

I, even I, am he that blotteth out thy transgressions for mine own sake, and will not remember thy sins. Put me in remembrance: let us plead together: declare thou, that thou mayest be justified.

Isaiah 43:25-26

In Ernest Hemingway's short story, **The Capital of the World,** he tells the story about a father and his teenage son who lived in Spain. Their relationship became strained, eventually shattered, and the son ran away from home. The father began a long journey in search of his lost and rebellious son. Finally, as a last resort he put an ad in the Madrid newspaper. His son's name was Paco, a very common name in Spain.

The ad simply read, "Dear Paco, meet me in front of the Madrid newspaper office tomorrow at noon. All is forgiven. I love you." As Hemingway writes, the next day at noon in front of the newspaper office there were 800 "Pacos" — all seeking forgiveness and reconcilation.

COME HOME...BE BLESSED

I have blotted out, as a thick cloud, thy transgressions, and, as a cloud, thy sins: return unto me; for I have redeemed thee.
Isaiah 44:22

God is in the forgiveness business. Today many people have trouble accepting the fact that God offers total forgiveness. Psalm 32:1 says, "Blessed is he whose transgression is forgiven, whose sin is covered." The Apostle Paul refers to this verse in Romans 4:6-8. This forgiveness includes the total erasing from His memory that sin was ever committed. He does this for His own sake, so He can bless us the way He wants.

If God doesn't remember that we have done anything wrong, then we should allow Him to erase it from our memory also. Smith Wigglesworth said, ***"Never look back if you want the power of God in your life."*** God's power is always propelling us forward.

NO MORE PARALYSIS

The story of the man with four crazy friends in Luke 5:17-26 is one of my favorites. When Jesus saw their faith, He told the man with paralysis, "Man, thy sins are forgiven thee." Jesus spoke to that man's deepest need. If Jesus calls you forgiven, you are totally forgiven and released from the condition and consequences of sin. You are redeemed. Then Jesus told him to "Arise!" The man got up and was totally healed of all paralysis.

This miracle caused the religious leaders much trouble. The rules and regulations of religion have paralyzed many people. However, when you get in the presence of Jesus, forgiveness and restoration are freely given. What a wonderful Jesus we have who forgives and heals! He is our Redeemer today.

REMIND ME OF THIS PROMISE

Because of Isaiah 43:25-26, we know God promises to blot out our transgressions and not remember our sins. God says remind me of this promise. This promise of forgiveness and our faith in this Word opens the door to God's goodness.

When we receive forgiveness and freely forgive ourselves and others our faith will work. God forgives us so radically and totally that He commands us to forgive others the same way. God's kind of forgiveness even erases the memory of all sin, failure, guilt, and accusation.

God loves and forgives like this and we, as His children and with His love nature, can and must do the same. Ephesians 4:32-5:2 makes this truth clear: "Let all bitterness, and wrath, and anger, and clamour, and evil speaking, be put away from you, with all malice: And be ye kind one to another, tenderhearted, forgiving one another, even as God for Christ's sake hath forgiven you. Be ye therefore followers of God, as dear children; And walk in love, as Christ also hath loved us...."

When we choose to forgive others, the weight of anger and bad feelings toward ourselves and others is gone. Remember 1 John 1:9 says that when we confess our sins, God is faithful and just to cleanse us from all unrighteousness. Instead of living life under the power of darkness and unforgiveness we can live in the light of God's love. "But if we walk in the light, as he is in the light, we have fellowship one with another, and the blood of Jesus Christ his Son cleanseth us from all sin," (1 John 1:7).

We acknowledge the power of the blood of Jesus cleanses us. It is the liquid love of God that will overflow into our lives to others. The blood gives us the power to live free from self condemnation and accusation. Righteousness is restored and our prayers will get results.

*And the prayer of faith shall save the sick,
and the Lord shall raise him up; and if he
have committed sins, they shall be forgiven
him. Confess your faults one to another,
and pray one for another, that ye may be
healed. The effectual fervent prayer of a
righteous man availeth much.*

James 5:15-16

Talk to your soul and let this praise continually flow from your lips:

*Bless the Lord, O my soul: and all that
is within me, bless his holy name. Bless
the Lord, O my soul, and forget not all
his benefits: Who forgiveth all thine
iniquities; who healeth all thy diseases;
Who redeemeth thy life from destruction;
who crowneth thee with lovingkindness
and tender mercies.*

Psalms 103:1-4

All is forgiven! God loves you! Now your faith is working, your prayers are heard and mountains will move.

A Confession of the Love of God

The love of God has been shed abroad in my heart by the Holy Ghost. I shall endeavor to let that love nature dominate me. I have God's love nature in my heart - in my spirit.

Therefore, I will not let my natural human reasoning dominate me. I refuse to allow the flesh to rule me.

I am going to walk in the spirit by walking in love. I am a lover and not a hater.

I will practice and exercise the fruit of love so it will grow and increase.

One way I will practice the God kind of love is by taking no thought for a suffered wrong.

I will practice thinking and saying the best of every person so my love can grow and develop, and I can be a blessing to many.

I will make the love of God my great quest in life, for then my love shall abound and God shall reap the glory!

I will walk in God's love. I will not criticize others because God's love works no ill to his neighbor.

When I am walking in God's love, I can claim God's best blessings in my life. I will be tenderhearted and forgiving; therefore I shall reap a blessing.

I will keep my tongue from speaking evil and pursue peace with every man.

I thank you Father that as I endeavor to grow in the fruit of love, you will help me be all that I can be in You!

From "Love - The Way to Victory"
by Kenneth E. Hagin

Prophecy from "The Love Walk"

Given by Kenneth E. Hagin, July 2003 - Rhema Campmeeting

Remember that it is written in the Word, be ye doers of the Word and not hearers only. For he that hears the Word and does not do it according to the Scripture has deceived himself. So, do not deceive yourself and walk away and not become a doer. But purpose in your heart, I am and I will be tomorrow and the next day as well a doer of the Word. Read the Word for yourself, act upon it. Take the scriptures that have been given this very night, write them down on a sheet of paper or on a card, read them almost constantly and act just like it is so and it will become so and become real in your life. You'll find that Satan will flee away. He'll take his hand off of you, he'll take his hand off of your loved one, he'll take his hand off of your affairs, and the blessings - the blessings shall flow and ye will know.

MARK HANKINS MINISTRIES PUBLICATIONS

SPIRIT-FILLED SCRIPTURE STUDY GUIDE

A comprehensive study of scriptures in over 120 different translations on topics such as: Redemption, Faith, Finances, Prayer and many more.

THE BLOODLINE OF A CHAMPION - THE POWER OF THE BLOOD OF JESUS

The blood of Jesus is the liquid language of love that flows from the heart of God and gives us hope in all circumstances. In this book, you will clearly see what the blood has done FOR US but also what the blood has done IN US as believers.

TAKING YOUR PLACE IN CHRIST

Many Christians talk about what they are trying to be and what they are going to be. This book is about who you are NOW as believers in Christ.

PAUL'S SYSTEM OF TRUTH

Paul's System of Truth reveals man's redemption in Christ, the reality of what happened from the cross to the throne and how it is applied for victory in life through Jesus Christ.

THE SECRET POWER OF JOY

If you only knew what happens in the Spirit when you rejoice, you would rejoice everyday. Joy is one of the great secrets of faith. This book will show you the importance of the joy of the Lord in a believer's life.

11:23 – THE LANGUAGE OF FAITH
Never under-estimate the power of one voice. Over 100 inspirational, mountain-moving quotes to "stir up" the spirit of faith in you.

LET THE GOOD TIMES ROLL
This book focuses on the five key factors to heaven on earth: The Holy Spirit, Glory, Faith, Joy, and Redemption. The Holy Spirit is a genius. If you will listen to Him, He will make you look smart.

THE POWER OF IDENTIFICATION WITH CHRIST
Learn how God identified us with Christ in His death, burial, resurrection, and seating in Heaven. The same identical life, victory, joy, and blessings that are In Christ are now in you. This is the glory and the mystery of Christianity – the power of the believer's identification with Christ.

REVOLUTIONARY REVELATION
This book provides excellent insight on how the spirit of wisdom and revelation is mandatory for believers to access their call, inheritance, and authority in Christ.

FAITH OPENS THE DOOR TO THE SUPERNATURAL

In this book you will learn how believing and speaking open the door to the supernatural.

NEVER RUN AT YOUR GIANT WITH YOUR MOUTH SHUT

We all face many giants in life that must be conquered before we can receive and do all that God has for us. Winning the War of words is necessary to win the fight of faith. So...Lift your voice!

THE SPIRIT OF FAITH

If you only knew what was on the other side of your mountain, you would move it! Having a spirit of faith is necessary to do the will of God and fulfill your destiny.

THE HOLY SPIRIT IS A GENIUS

The Holy Spirit takes what Jesus has done **FOR** us and makes it a reality **IN** us. The Holy Spirit takes all your receiving from God to a whole new dimension.

GOD'S HEALING WORD by Trina Hankins

Trina's testimony and a practical guide to receiving healing through meditating on the Word of God. This guide includes: testimonies, practical teaching, Scriptures & confessions, and a CD with Scriptures & confessions (read by Mark Hankins).

Notes:

Notes:

Notes:

Notes:

Notes:

Bibliography

Amplified Bible. Zondervan Publishing House, Grand Rapids, Michigan, 1972.

Barclay, William. *The New Testament, A New Translation.* Collins, London, England, 1968.

Drummond, Henry. *The Greatest Thing in the World.* Public Domain.

Hagin, Kenneth. *Love the Way to Victory.* Faith Library Publications, 1994.

Hayford, Jack W. *Spirit-Filled Life Bible.* Thomas Nelson, Inc. Nashville, Tennessee, 1991.

Johnson, Clarence. *The Cotton Patch Version of Paul's Epistles.* Word Books, Waco, TX, 1976.

Jordan, Clarence. *The Cotton Patch Version of Paul's Epistles.* Associated Press, New York, New York, 1968.

Peterson, Eugene. *The Message, The Bible in Contemporary Language.* Nav Press Publishing Group, Colorado Springs, CO, 2003.

Phillips, J.B. *The New Testament in Modern English.* The Macmillan Company, New York, New York, 1958.

Simmons, Bryan. *The Passion Translation.* Broadstreet Publishing Group, LLC; Compact edition, 2018.

Taylor, Ken. *The Living Bible.* Tyndale House Publishers, Wheaton, Illinois, 1971.

Williams, Charles G. *The New Testament.* Moody Press, Chicago, Illinois, 1978.

Wuest, Kenneth S. *The New Testament, An Expanded Translation.* William B. Eerdmans Publishing Company, Grand Rapids, Michigan, 1981.

INTERESTED IN GOING DEEPER?

"THE GREATEST THING IN THE WORLD"
BY HENRY DRUMMOND

LOVE THE SECRET TO SUCCESS (4 CD SET)

FOR A FULL LIST OF RESOURCES,
VISIT US ONLINE AT WWW.MARKHANKINS.ORG
OR CALL OUR OFFICES AT 318-767-2001!

DOWNLOAD THE APP
TV BROADCAST + RADIO PROGRAM + ITNERARY + MORE

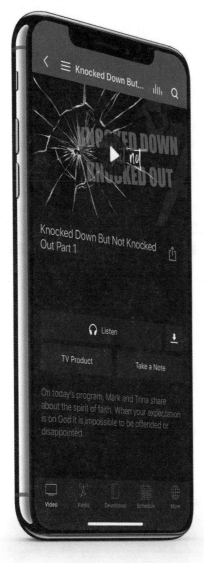

SIMPLY SEARCH
"MARK HANKINS MINISTRIES"
IN THE APP STORE

CONNECT WITH US

P.O. BOX 12863 ALEXANDRIA, LA 71315 + 318.767.2001

 MARKHANKINSMINISTRIES1123

 MARKHANKINS1123

 MARKHANKINS1123

 MARK HANKINS MINISTRIES TV

 WWW.MARKHANKINS.ORG